KEEP YOUR LOVE ON!

KYLO

STUDY SERIES

DANNY SILK

KEEP YOUR LOVE ON!
Connection, Communication & Boundaries
Study Series, Study Guide
Copyright © 2014 by Danny Silk

FIRST EDITION

Cover Design © Samuel Nudds & Linda Lee
Interior Design © Vision Tank & Renee Evans

ISBN 978-0-9888984-4-8
Printed in the United States

CONTENTS

INTRODUCTION
How to use the *Keep Your Love On! Study Guide*

The *Keep Your Love On! Study Guide* is designed to be used with the *Keep Your Love On!* book and either the audio or DVD series. Each lesson opens with reading a book chapter, listening to an audio session, and/or viewing a DVD session, and then moves into the following sections:

Study Guide Unit Outline

Core Concepts
Identify the key terms and concepts of the book chapter, audio session, and/or DVD session.

Think About It
Answer questions designed to help you apply the Core Concepts to your life and relationships.

Real Life Scenario
Consider a scenario, taken from Danny's personal ministry and counseling sessions, that depicts a common relational problem.

What *is* the Problem?
Use the Core Concepts to identify and understand the problem in the Real-Life Scenario.

A Word from Danny
Danny gives his wisdom to help you understand the problem and offer a solution.

KYLO in Action
Encourages you to take action on what you've learned in the lesson.

LESSON 1
Powerful People, Powerful Relationships

 Unfortunately, most of us did not grow up to be powerful people. If you were blessed to have parents who taught you to be responsible for your choices, then you should go home and thank them. It's a rare gift. Most people don't know that they can be powerful, or even that they ought to be. They are trained from a young age that someone else is responsible for their decisions, and all they have to do is comply and obey. This sets them up to struggle in multiple aspects of life, particularly with building healthy  relationships.

(*Keep Your Love On!*, page 20)

Core Concepts

Read Chapter 1 of the *Keep Your Love On* book, listen to Session 1 of the audio series, and/or watch DVD Session 1. Then fill in the blanks below.

Powerless People

- Powerless people use powerless language. They say, "I can't. I'll try. I have to."

- The driving force of powerless people is _____ and anxiety, and they create anxiety-driven environments around them.

- A powerless person acts like a _____ because he or she believes everything and everyone else is more powerful than he or she is.

Powerless Relationships

- Powerless people create a classic relational dynamic called _____.

- Victims look for a _____ to make them feel happy and safe, and a "bad guy" to _____ for their problems.

- Powerless people try to _____ one another instead of themselves.

Powerful People

- Powerful people say things like, "I can. I will. I am."

- The driving force of powerful people is peace and love, and they create environments of safety and _____ around them.

- Powerful people are _____ for their own happiness.

Powerful Relationships

- A powerful relationship is built on the decision, "I _____"

- Powerful people require other people's _____ and expect them to manage themselves in a relationship.

Core Concepts Key Words:

respect	fear	victim	triangulation	rescuer`
blame	control	freedom	responsible	choose

The Triangulation Cycle

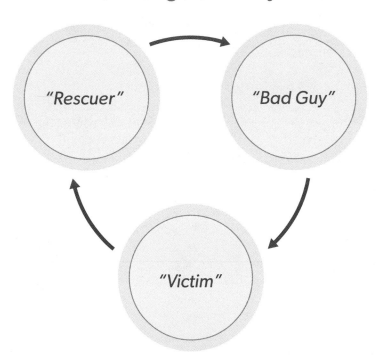

Victim: looks for a rescuer to make him/her feel safe and happy

Rescuer: takes responsibility for someone else's life in an attempt to feel powerful

Bad Guy: uses control and intimidation to protect him/her or get someone to meet his/her needs

1) Think about 3 different relationships in your life. Would you say the foundation of these relationships is, "I choose you?" Why or why not?

2) In those 3 relationships, have you tried to manage and control the other person's side of the relationship at all? How?

3) Have you observed or participated in the triangulation cycle in your relationships? If so, which role did you typically play—Victim, Bad Guy, or Rescuer? Explain.you? What would "powerful" sound like in those situations?

4) Who is the most powerful person you know? What characteristics do you admire in him or her?

5) Do you think of yourself primarily as powerful or powerless? What are some steps you can take to becoming more powerful?

Lauren and Ella

"Danny, I just don't know what to do," Lauren sighed, shaking her head. "My four-year-old daughter, Ella, is normally so sweet and fun. But a few months ago she started throwing the most horrible tantrums in public. It's happened at church, the supermarket, the beach, the park… If I ask her to do something she doesn't want to do, she morphs into this screaming, flailing, 'Out-of-control Ella' and it is simply impossible to reason with her. It's so embarrassing. All I can do is stop what we're doing, pack up, and leave. Do you know how many times I've left my basket full of groceries because I am dragging my child to the car?"

"That's tough," Danny agreed. "Can I ask if she's trying to pull this behavior with anyone else?"

"No, that's what is especially frustrating. She never does it with my husband or her grandparents or preschool teacher. Just me! What can I do with her? Help!"

? What *is* the Problem?

Would you say Ella and Lauren are acting powerful or powerless in this scenario? Explain.

What are some things Lauren and Ella need to do to be powerful and build a powerful relationship?

A Word from Danny

Lauren is acting powerless in the face of her daughter's disrespectful behavior. As a result, Ella has learned that "Out-of-control Ella" is a great way to get her mom to move her boundaries. Lauren needs to show Ella that in their relationship, both people need to control themselves and be respectful.

Lauren can start acting powerful—and requiring Ella to be powerful—by setting and enforcing clear limits with Ella. The simplest way to set a limit is to offer a choice. For example, when Ella starts to go into "out-of-control" mode, Lauren can say, "Hey Ella—do you want to be fun and keep shopping with me, or do you want to go to your room?" If Ella continues to be disrespectful, then Lauren will need to make sure that Ella ends up in her room. Lauren can plan for her husband or a friend to pick up Ella and take her home to her room so she doesn't have to abandon her grocery cart.

Ella may need a few opportunities to learn that Lauren will no longer be manipulated by "Out-of-control Ella" and that she needs to manage herself and be respectful in their relationship. But if Laura leads in being powerful and following through on what she says, Ella will learn to be powerful too.

> Powerful people bring to the table the very best of who they are. Being powerful means you're able to say *yes* when you mean *yes*, and *no* when you mean *no*. It's not about being the loudest or strongest in the room. It's about knowing how to manage yourself toward your goal. Remember: the best relationships are when two powerful people partner together with the goal of connection.

♥ KYLO in Action

1) What you are going to do this week to become more powerful? Give an example of powerful language you will use and powerful behavior you will practice.

2) How are you managing yourself and your side of relationships this week? Explain.

Remember: *Keep Your Love On!*

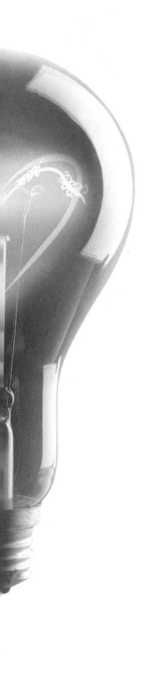

LESSON 2
Turn Your Love On

 Until you commit to the goal of connection, all the relational tools in the world are not going to help you. It's only when you decide to take responsibility to pursue connection that you will discover just why you need these tools. It's only when you commit to moving toward someone that you will seek the knowledge and skills  necessary to reach them.

(Keep Your Love On!, page 45)

Core Concepts

Read Chapter 2 of the *Keep Your Love On* book, listen to Session 2 of the audio series, and/or watch DVD Session 2. Then fill in the blanks below.

Goal of Relationship

- Every relationship has one of two goals: _____ or disconnection.

- If your goal is disconnection, you work to keep a safe _____ from the other person.

- If there's a _____ in your relationship, the first step is not to fix it, but to restore connection.

- When you "keep your love on," you _____ to move toward the other person, even in the face of hurt or mistakes.

- In a powerful relationship, each person takes _____ for their commitment to pursuing the goal of connection, regardless of what the other person does.

Building Connection with the 5 Love Languages

*adapted from the book **The 5 Love Languages** by Gary Chapman*

- Every person usually has one primary way that they receive and show love—one type of _____ that fills up their "love tanks."

- It is essential to show love to people in their love language so they can feel connected in a relationship.

- If you have the _____ love language, you need regular physical affection to keep your love tank filled.

- Acts of Service people feel anxious if you aren't _____ .

- If you are a Gifts person, you feel loved when someone gives you a gift that says, "I know you."

- If someone feels loved through your interest in him or her, then he or she must be a _____ person.

- Encouragement feels like love to the _____ person, while criticism increases his or her anxiety.

Core Concepts Key Words:

choose/commit	fuel	connection	touch	responsibility
problem	distance	quality time	serving/helping	words of affirmation

Think About It

1) Are there any relationships in which you have lost the goal of connection and allowed distance to become normal?

2) If you have made a safe distance the goal of your relationship, what is one way you can move toward that person?

3) Can you identify your top two love languages? What are they? What makes you feel loved?

4) Do you know the love languages of your closest friends and family members? Are you successfully hitting the target that makes them feel loved? If not, are you willing to communicate with them to determine the target?

5) How do you "paint a target" for those in your closest relationships to communicate to you in your love language? Are the messages you are sending to them getting the appropriate responses?

Real Life Scenario

Clark and Tina

After nearly a decade of marriage, Clark and Tina still "love each other to bits," and are thrilled to be expecting their first child. Yet when they came to see Danny, they admitted they didn't feel as connected as they wanted to be.

"What makes you feel most connected to Clark?" Danny asked Tina.

"Probably when we're cuddling on the couch watching a movie," she replied.

"And how often do you guys do that?"

"Maybe once a week or so," Tina shrugged. "I wish it was more."

"But we cuddle in bed some mornings, too," Clark jumped in.

"Only when I initiate it, and that hasn't happened for months," Tina said, shaking her head in disappointment. "Clark's been sleeping in the guest bedroom lately."

"I have insomnia!" Clark said, frustrated. "I get too hot sleeping in the bed with her, and sometimes she snores. If I can't get a good night's sleep, I can't function at work, which stresses me out and makes it even harder to sleep. With a baby on the way, I really can't afford to lose my job."

"Well, it sounds like cuddling isn't as important to you, Clark," Danny observed. "What would you say makes you feel connected to Tina?"

Clark thought for a moment. "It means a lot when she encourages me. I remember once hearing her praise me to some friends of hers and I felt like a million bucks."

"So did you tell her how much that meant to you?" Danny asked.

"Yeah, sort of," Clark said, shifting uncomfortably. "I mean, I thanked her. But it would feel wrong to ask her to do that more."

? What *is* the Problem?

What would you say are Clark's and Tina's primary love languages?

_____

_____

_____

What would you suggest to Clark and Tina to improve their communication with one another in their love languages and strengthen their connection?

_____

_____

_____

_____

💬 A Word from Danny

Tina's top love language is Touch—affection makes her feel connected to her husband. And Words of Affirmation from Tina make Clark feel loved. But neither of them is doing a great job of showing one another that they need a steady flow of touch and affirmation in their relationship. As a result, they are not "feeling the love," and this is creating anxiety, disappointment, and frustration that weaken their connection.

In a powerful relationship, both people have the right and responsibility to communicate their emotional needs to one another in a way that provides a clear "target" for the other person to hit. For example, Tina might say, "Clark, I feel so loved when you cuddle in bed with me and show me affection throughout the day." With this great information, Clark can work on a plan to get a good night's sleep that doesn't require his wife to do without the touch she needs. And Clark needs to be vulnerable and say, "Tina, I really *need* your affirmation. It brings me so much strength and helps me be the man that I want to be for you and our family." This message will alert Tina to consistently look for ways she can praise and build up her man.

As these two become powerful in communicating and meeting one another's emotional needs, they will a build a connection that will help them weather any challenge—from sleepless nights to raising their family and more!

> ❝ 'I love you very much' is a simple message, but unfortunately it's one of the best-kept secrets among people who care for each other. Knowing how the people around you hear and feel love will help drop the anxiety and achieve your goal of connection. ❞

KYLO in Action

1) What is the goal in your close relationships—a close connection or a safe distance? Are you building a skill set to control the distance between you, or to move toward them and keep your love on no matter what? How?

2) Think of 3 people who are important to you. Write down one thing you can do this week to speak to each of those people in his or her love language and send the message, "I love you very much and this relationship is important to me."

3) Are you powerful in communicating your emotional needs clearly in your closest relationships? Do you "paint targets" for one another? If not, sit down face to face with one of these people. Take turns telling one another, "I feel loved when you…" Then take that great information and find ways to hit those targets!

Remember: *Keep Your Love On!*

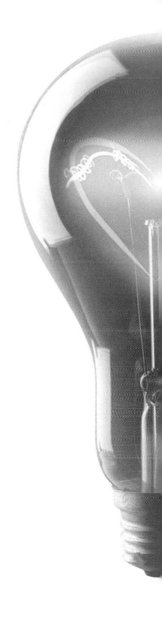

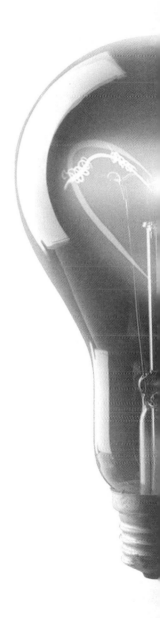

LESSON 3

The Battle Between Fear and Love

> Fear and love are enemies. They come from two opposing kingdoms. Fear comes from the enemy, who would like nothing more than to keep you permanently disconnected and isolated. Love comes from God, who is always working to heal and restore your connection with Him and other people and bring you into healthy, life-giving relationships.

(Keep Your Love On!, page 52)

Core Concepts

Read Chapter 3 of the *Keep Your Love On* book, listen to Session 3 of the audio series, and/or watch DVD Session 3. Then fill in the blanks below.

Fear vs. Love

* The battle between fear and love is a _____ battle.

* Fear and love have opposite agendas, and opposite strategies for achieving them. They cannot _____ in a person, relationship, or culture.

Fear Reacts & Seeks Control

* We usually develop three instinctive _____ to the threat of pain: fight, flight, or freeze.

* Fear teaches you that it's your job to _____ people through intimidation and the threat of punishment.

* If you believe that you can be controlled, you will also believe that you can control _____.

* When you operate out of fear, you create a _____ of fear around you.

Love Responds & Seeks Connection

* In order to respond with love, you must _____ your mind to think, your will to choose, and your body to obey.

* You cannot control other people. The only person you can control—on a good day—is _____.

- To align yourself with love, your number-one priority in relationships must be building and protecting _____.

- Connection drives _____ away. Losing connection invites that powerful, destructive force to come back.

Core Concepts Key Words:

others	connection	yourself	culture	reactions
spiritual	fear	train	control	coexist

Think About It

1) People generally develop three classic reactions to the threat of pain—fight, flight, or freeze. How do you typically react? Explain.

2) How do your reactions affect your relationships?

3) What are some examples of responding to a relational issue vs. reacting to one?

4) Do you believe you can control other people or that other people can control you? How do you react or respond when someone is trying to control or manipulate you?

5) Do people in your life feel safe to be vulnerable with you? Do you feel safe being vulnerable with them? If not, what would need to happen for you to create a safe place together?

Martin and Elsa

"Elsa!"

"I'm in the kitchen, Martin," Elsa called to her husband, her voice heavy with exhaustion as she wiped off the countertop with a paper towel. They'd just arrived home from a grueling international trip, and she was as jet-lagged and cranky as her infant son, who she'd just put down for his nap.

"Why are you cleaning the kitchen?" Martin's tall frame appeared in the doorway, his tone stern. "I told you we needed to go to the grocery store."

"I know…" Elsa's voice was soft but tense as she continued to clean. "I don't want to put food in a dirty kitchen." The wail of their nine-month-old son pierced the air. "Can you check on him, please? I just put him down."

"What? It's too early!" Martin's voice rose in exasperation. "We have to get him on schedule or he won't sleep tonight!"

Elsa's mouth tightened as her blood pressure rose. "I know, but he was so tired," she explained, marshaling her tension to speak calmly. "I just couldn't let him keep crying."

"Well, now he's just going to cry all night!" Martin yelled in frustration. "And we won't have time to go shopping if he's napping!"

"I can stay here while he sleeps if you have to go right now," Elsa snapped quietly. "I made a list for the grocery store. It's on the table."

"I don't want a list!" Martin roared. "I told you I wanted you to come with me! I need your help!"

"Martin, please…" Elsa ground out. "We're both beyond tired. If you don't want to go, you can stay here, and I'll go do the shopping."

"Why can't you just do what I asked in the first place?" Martin threw his arms in the air.

"Martin, I really don't need this right now," said Elsa, her voice breaking. Tossing the paper towel in the trash, she ran to the bedroom, slammed the door, and collapsed on the bed in tears.

? What *is* the Problem?

Would you say Martin and Elsa are reacting or responding to stress in this scenario? How might this affect their connection? Explain.

How could Elsa and Martin better align themselves with love and respond to stress and one another more powerfully?

A Word from Danny

Martin and Elsa are both reacting to the stress of trying to meet certain needs while feeling exhausted and powerless. Martin's instinctive reaction is to "fight" with yelling and intimidation, which provokes Elsa to "flee." This kind of disrespectful exchange only heightens their anxiety and attacks their trust and connection.

Martin and Elsa need to agree that nothing—not exhaustion, the screaming baby, or one another's actions—gives them permission to stop controlling themselves and start trying to control one another. No matter what is going on, they are powerful people who get to choose how they will respond—with love, respect, and self-control. No matter what, they are committed to moving toward one another and protecting their connection.

This couple should agree to start training themselves to check in with their hearts when they start to feel anxiety, pain, anger, or frustration. They can stop and ask, "Do I feel powerless right now? If so, why? Instead of trying to control someone or something else in this situation, what is something I can do to control myself and respond here?" For example, Martin might be able to see, "I'm feeling powerless about getting the shopping done, but it needs to get done.

Elsa's too exhausted and the baby has to sleep. Instead of trying to control her, is there something else I can do to reach my goal? Can the shopping wait? Can I call a friend?"

Martin and Elsa can also give one another permission to be powerful and confront if they start to see "fight," "flight," or "freeze" behavior. For example, instead of being passive in this conflict, Elsa could say, "Martin, I'm sorry I can't go to the store right now. I know you're frustrated, but I feel disrespected when you speak to me that way. I need to feel safe that you won't punish or try to control me when I can't do something that you want."

As both Elsa and Martin take responsibility to manage their own anxiety and make powerful choices to move toward one another, they will win the battle of fear and love.

> God's number one goal with us is connection, and nothing—neither pain nor death—will prevent Him from moving toward us and responding to us with love.

KYLO in Action

1. Ask yourself these simple questions: "Do I believe I can control other people? How am I doing at controlling me instead of trying to control others?"

2. Now ask, "What can I do to better control *me*? What can I do to protect connection when I feel hurt or afraid?"

3. Make these commitments aloud:
- *It's my job to control myself. I do not get to control other people.*
- *My number-one goal and priority in relationships is building and protecting connection.*

> The choice to pursue the goal of connection will bring you right up against the real conflict that lies at the core of every relationship. It is a spiritual battle—a heart battle—drawn between the two most powerful forces that drive us: fear and love. If you want to be a powerful person capable of building intimate relationship, then it is absolutely vital that you learn how these forces operate and align yourself with love.

Remember: *Keep Your Love On!*

LESSON 4
Building Healthy Relationships

Healthy relationships truly are the most valuable, meaningful, and satisfying of human experiences. But what are the qualities that make up a healthy relational connection? If you don't know, then you won't be able to assess whether or not your relational practices are helping to build and strengthen a connection.

(*Keep Your Love On!*, page 62)

Read Chapter 4 of the *Keep Your Love On* book, listen to Session 4 of the audio series, and/or watch DVD Session 4. Then fill in the blanks below.

Seven Pillars of Healthy Relationships

Foundation

- The foundation of a healthy relationship is _____ acceptance and love, which says, "You get to be you and I get to be me in this relationship."

Love

- Love creates a place of _____, connection, peace, and trust. If I have loved you well, you will feel safe, valued, connected, nourished, protected, pursued, known, and understood.

Honor

- True honor is the practice of two _____ people putting one another before themselves, empowering one another, working together to meet one another's needs, and adjusting as necessary to move together toward the shared goals of the relationship. It's calling out the _____ in one another.

Self-Control

- Self-control means that you can _____ yourself what to do, and make yourself do it. Self-control is at the core of being a powerful person.

Responsibility

- Responsibility means the ability to respond. It is the capacity to face any situation and make powerful choices that are _____ with who you say you are.

Truth

- You build _____ and intimacy as you exchange the truth about what is going on inside you.

Faith

- Faith is built in a relationship as two people commit to keep _____ as their ultimate source, ultimate comforter, and ultimate authority.

Vision

- You build the pillar of vision as you share the knowledge of one another's identity and calling, as well as your joint vision, and _____ one another of these things on a regular basis.

Shalom

- When you lay a firm foundation of unconditional love and acceptance and build the pillars of love, honor, self-control, responsibility, truth, faith, and vision in your relationship, you raise a structure that can protect and cultivate an environment of shalom, which is the reality of God's _____ of righteousness, peace, and joy expressed in your life.

| God | safety | remind | powerful | trust |
| kingdom | best | tell | consistent | unconditional |

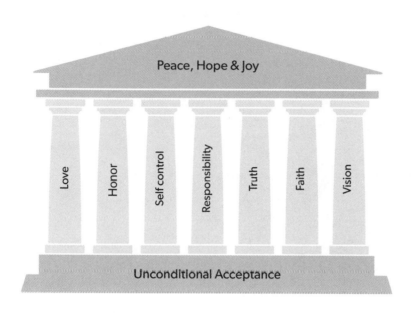

Think About It

1) Would you say that your closest relationships are built on the foundation of unconditional love and acceptance? Why or why not?

2) Looking at the 7 pillars, which pillars do you feel you have established in your relationships? Which pillars do you want to improve?

3) What are some examples of how to practice honor in your relationships?

4) How could you be intentional about looking to God as the ultimate source of your comfort and authority?

5) What is your vision for your personal relationships? In what ways are you working toward this?

Real Life Scenario

Rita and Monica

For the fifth time in the last fifteen minutes, Rita felt her phone buzz in her jacket pocket. Sighing, she pulled the phone out and saw she had five texts waiting—all from Monica.

"Hey, I'm borrowing your sweater…maybe we can clean out your closet when you get back?"

"Did you take those vitamins I got for you?"

"I signed us up for that new spinning class at the gym tomorrow. 10 AM. You're gonna love it!"

"Circled some great jobs in the paper today for you."

"Okay, I'm reading this article about online dating…Let's talk about it. I will help you fill out your profile!"

A wave of anger surged through Rita. "This is too much!" she said aloud, stuffing her phone back in her pocket.

It had been three months since Monica had graciously invited Rita to move in with her family until she could get back on her feet after a tragic divorce. At first, Rita had felt nothing but gratitude for Monica's generosity and enjoyed spending lots of quality time with her childhood friend. She had poured out her heart about her failed marriage to Monica, who had been more than happy to listen and offer endless counsel to help Rita understand her "issues" and move on. But for the last month or so, Rita had found herself struggling with negative feelings provoked by Monica's relentless efforts to help and fix her.

Yet today, for the hundredth time, Rita decided to talk herself out of these negative feelings rather than admit them to Monica. She told herself that Monica was just trying to help, and that she would feel horribly guilty if she said anything that sounded ungrateful when Monica had done so much for her. "Just put up with it," she sighed to herself. "It won't be forever."

? What *is* the Problem?

Which of the seven pillars—love, honor, responsibility, self-control, truth, faith, and vision would you say are weak in Rita and Monica's friendship?

_____

_____

_____

What should Rita and Monica do to help build and strengthen these pillars?

_____

_____

_____

_____

💬 A Word from Danny

Let's start with the foundation of Rita and Monica's friendship. Despite Rita's vulnerability and Monica's demonstrations of "help," this relationship is not built on unconditional love and acceptance. Rita doesn't feel accepted by Monica; she feels like a project. As a result, Rita believes, "I don't get to be me in this relationship."

Without unconditional love and acceptance, it's no surprise that we don't see many of the seven pillars established here. Instead of a safe, loving connection, we see a codependent, fear-based connection. Instead of two powerful people acting with honor, there is dishonor because of Rita's powerlessness in allowing Monica to push the boundaries around her time, plans, and possessions. By definition, Rita's powerlessness is lacking in self-control and responsibility, and she is also preventing the exchange of truth by hiding her feelings from Monica. And as in any codependent relationship, there's a good chance that faith and vision are lacking here. After all, God is the only one responsible to "fix" us. Anytime we step into that role in another person's life or allow someone to step into that role for us, we are not being ourselves, we're not letting others be themselves, and we're not letting God be God.

If Rita and Monica want to build a strong, healthy relationship, then they both need to commit to being powerful and requiring one another to be powerful. Rita needs to tell Monica the truth about how she is feeling and set clear boundaries around her time and activities so that Monica is not working harder on Rita's life than Rita is. Connecting to God and their God-given purpose and identity will help them clarify the boundary lines around their lives so they can take responsibility to manage themselves and not one another. As these two powerful ladies work together to hold up their end of the relationship, they will invite peace and joy to fill their connection.

KYLO in Action

Write down one thing you can do to be intentional about strengthening the seven pillars of healthy relationships in your life:

1. Love:

2. Honor:

3. Self-Control:

4. Responsibility:

5. Truth:

6. Faith:

7. Vision:

Remember: *Keep Your Love On!*

LESSON 5
Communication: Exchanging the Truth Inside

Communication exposes what is going on inside the human heart. Jesus said, "For out of the abundance of the heart the mouth speaks." If your heart, your internal reality is governed by fear, then you are going to express that through your body language, facial expressions, words and tone. Conversely, if your heart is governed by faith, hope, and love you will release this reality through what you say and how you say it.

(*Keep Your Love On!*, page 81)

Core Concepts

Read Chapter 5 of the *Keep Your Love On* book, listen to Session 5 of the audio series, and/or watch DVD Session 5. Then fill in the blanks below.

The Goal of Communication

- The first goal in communication is to _____ the other person, not to agree with him or her.

- The greatest skill you could ever cultivate in a relationship is to _____ well, especially in a disagreement.

- It's your job to communicate what's going on inside of _____, not try to explain what's going on inside someone else.

- Listening well and seeking understanding sends the message, "I care about you," and decreases _____.

Communication Styles

- _____ communicators attempt to convince the world that everyone else is more important than they are. They say things like, "Whatever you want. I'm fine. Don't worry about me."

- The aggressive communicator believes, "I _____ ; you don't."

- If you are a _____ communicator, then you use sarcasm, innuendos, veiled threats, and manipulation to communicate your needs.

- _____ communicators believe, "You matter and so do I." They require conversations to involve two powerful people, and say things like, "I would be glad to listen as long as this conversation is _____."

Levels of Communication

- Many people only feel safe in superficial conversations, exchanging only facts and chichés, since they require no vulnerability or connection.

- The next level of communication involves sharing opinions. This is where disagreement can begin to happen.

- The deepest level of communication involves sharing feelings and _____. This is what builds intimacy and a heart-to-heart connection.

Core Concepts Key Words:

respectful	needs	matter	understand	passive
assertive	anxiety	you	listen	passive-aggressive

1) If you never really learn to value and understand what's going on inside you, how can you value and understand what is going on inside another person?

2) If you don't know yourself, how can you get to know another person—someone with a completely different experience and perspective—and value the truth of who they are?

3) When you are having a disagreement with someone, do you find yourself trying to tell the other person about what's going on inside of him/her instead of telling the person what's going on inside of you?

4) Which communication style have you primarily adopted — passive, aggressive, passive-aggressive, or assertive? Explain.

5) Do you feel comfortable and safe communicating your needs in your closest relationships? Why or why not?

> One of the most helpful things you can remember is to keep *understanding* as the goal of all effective communication. Remember to tell others about you and allow them to tell you about them. Reveal your heart whenever you communicate.

Real Life Scenario

Josh and Alan

"I think that's everything," Josh said, placing the steaming bowl of mashed potatoes on the Thanksgiving table. As his family eagerly dug into the feast, Josh couldn't help but notice with growing alarm that Alan, his nearly 400-pound brother, was heaping his plate higher than anyone else. Try as he did to ignore it, Josh kept glancing over at Alan throughout the entire meal and noting how much and how quickly he was eating.

While the rest of the family enjoyed dessert, Josh wrestled with the idea of whether or not he should say anything to his brother about losing weight. His previous attempts to broach the subject had only resulted in Alan getting defensive and harsh, which made the rest of their time together miserable.

After helping to clear the table, the two brothers headed up to Josh's "man cave" to watch football. During the half-time show, Alan got up and left the room, saying, "Be right back, Bro." He soon returned with a couple of beers and a bag of chips.

"Wow," Josh couldn't help saying. "How are you still hungry?"

"It's football!" Alan responded enthusiastically. "Gotta have a snack with football."

"Even after Thanksgiving dinner?" Josh pressed, his tone failing to hide his annoyance.

"Dude, that's the point of Thanksgiving," Alan grunted.

Josh held his tongue and tried to focus on the game, but the sound of his brother eating was so grating that he finally stood up and looked directly at his brother.

"Alan, this has got to stop. Look at you. You are seriously out of control. Are you trying to kill yourself?"

Alan's eyes flashed at Josh in anger. After a long tense moment, he stood up to leave the room.

"Back off, Josh," he said firmly. "You know we're not talking about this. Period. I could think of some things to tell you to fix, but I keep my mouth shut."

? What *is* the Problem?

How would you describe Josh's and Alan's communication styles?

How could Josh improve his approach to communicating with his brother?

💬 A Word from Danny

Josh is experiencing high levels of anxiety over his brother's health. No doubt he has genuine love for Alan, but with fear driving his communication, he comes across as aggressive: "I need you to stop blowing up your life, now!" This sends the message that his needs matter more than Alan's. Josh is also being disrespectful in his "Let me tell you about you" approach. In the face of aggression and disrespect, it's no wonder Alan got defensive and walked out.

Alan is acting like his health problem is not really a problem, which means he's probably not looking for a solution. If Josh wants to send a message that his brother will be likely to hear, it won't be a solution to a problem his brother doesn't have; it will be about the state of their heart-to-heart connection. Chances are these two are not very connected thanks to disrespectful conversations and anxiety eroding their relationship. Josh needs to be vulnerable and show Alan his heart by saying, "Hey, I love you and our relationship is really important to me. I'm feeling disconnected, and I'm willing to do whatever it takes to reconnect." He will need to be willing to clean up any messes he's made by being disrespectful and invite Alan to rebuild trust. Then he will need to be committed to creating a safe place—through listening well, showing that he cares about Alan's feelings and needs, and demonstrating that he will never again try to fix or control him—for Alan to share what's going on inside.

When their connection grows strong enough, it may be that Alan will volunteer to share about his health issues on his own. Or Josh may find a moment where he can crack his heart open to Alan and say, "Hey, I love you so much. I don't want to control you or fix you. But I need you to know that what you're doing to yourself scares me." Only with persistent vulnerability, respect, and care will these brothers can create a relationship where these deep issues are safe enough to come out and be addressed.

 KYLO in Action

1. Only those who value and understand themselves can value and understand others. Do you feel you value and understand yourself? Explain.

2. Only those who can communicate honestly with themselves can communicate honestly with others. Do you feel you can communicate honestly with yourself? How about communicating your needs to others? Explain.

3) Start practicing the skills of assertive communication by:

a) Paying attention to your thoughts, feelings, and needs and respecting their value.

b) Start doing the same for other people.

c) Check yourself when you are tempted to invalidate someone's experience or heart.

d) Listen to understand in a conversation—especially to understand what a person is feeling and what he or she needs.

e) Seek healing from past experiences that have led you to fear the truth of your heart and become a passive, aggressive, or passive-aggressive communicator. Be real with yourself. If you start slipping into your old styles of communication, then do what needs to be done make things right.

f) Write down your thoughts, process, and progress.

Remember: *Keep Your Love On!*

LESSON 6
The Trust Cycle

 In a respectful relationship, each person understands, "I am responsible to know what is going on inside me and communicate it to you. I do not expect you to know it, nor will I allow you to assume that you know it. And I will not make assumptions about what is going on inside you."

(Keep Your Love On!, page 100)

Read Chapter 6 of the *Keep Your Love On* book, listen to Session 6 of the audio series, and/or watch DVD Session 6. Then fill in the blanks below.

The Trust Cycle

- Our deepest need is to _____ and be loved by other human beings and engage in lasting relational bonds.

- Our ability to meet this need develops as we consistently complete trust cycles in the context of a _____ connection.

- A trust cycle is completed when:

  o There is a need

  o The need is _____

  o There is a _____ to the need

  o The need is _____

  o Comfort is received

The Mistrust Cycle

- The trust cycle can break down at any point, which creates a cycle of mistrust. Trust is damaged if:

  o People fail to _____ and express their needs

  o The other person does not respond to the need or responds in a _____ way

  o The need is ultimately not satisfied

I Message

- Trust is built through the exchange of truth. You need to communicate your needs clearly so that the other person is able to meet them.

- The best tool for telling another person about you is an "_____."

- It begins with "I _____," not "I think."

- It is designed to let other people know about what is happening _____ you, not for you to tell them what you think about them or what they should do.

Core Concepts Key Words:

i message	satisfied	relational	response	inside
love	identify	expressed	negative	feel

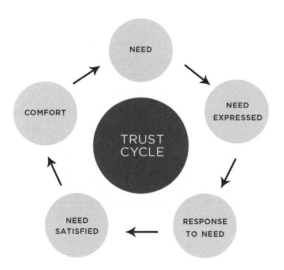

1) Learning to communicate needs is an important step to establish trust in a relationship. On a scale of 1-10, how well do you feel you communicate your needs right now, with 10 being the best? Explain.

2) Do you ever feel that you have to manipulate people or situations in order to get your needs met? Do you identify any "counterfeits" to intimacy in your life, such as using money, food, or sex to try to meet your needs through control? If so, explain.

3) Can you think of an experience where you received the message, "Your feelings and needs are invalid and unimportant?" How did you respond to this experience?

4) Have you ever had a confrontation where you felt it was your job to tell the other person about what was going on inside of him or her instead of what was going on inside of you? How did it affect the conversation or the relationship?

5) Practice constructing an "I message." Use a situation in your life as an example.

"I feel _____ when _____ and

               emotion   describe experience

I need to feel _____."

                                         emotion

> The level of communication we need to reach in order to build a strong relational connection is the level where we express our needs to one another. It's no mistake that this is exactly where the trust cycle begins.

Real Life Scenario

Justin and Briana

Justin whipped his car into Briana's driveway. Glancing at his dashboard, he saw that he was only thirty minutes late to pick her up. He knew his fiancée would probably throw out a few passive-aggressive comments about his lateness and be anxious the whole drive to the airport, but oh well—she knew cutting it down to the wire was his style. She hadn't even tried to call or text him to tell him to hurry up.

Running up to the door, he opened it without knocking and called, "Hey, I'm here! My meeting this morning went a little long, sorry...Babe?"

The house was silent, dark, and apparently empty. Frantically, Justin pulled out his phone to call her.

"Hey," Briana answered, her voice calm.

"I'm here at the house to pick you up. Where are you?"

"I'm at the airport. I called a taxi."

"What?" Adrenaline spiked through Justin. "What's wrong? Why didn't you wait for me?"

"Well, I knew you'd be late and I didn't want to miss our flight like last time."

"So you just went without me?!" Justin barked. "Why didn't you call or text me?"

"I've already told you that missing flights stresses me out. I did what I had to do to make sure that didn't happen again."

Gritting his teeth, Justin headed for his car. "Fine," he clipped. "See you on the plane."

? What *is* the Problem?

Are Justin and Briana's actions and communication helping to build a trust cycle, or a mistrust cycle?

How could this couple improve in communicating their feelings and needs to one another?

💬 A Word from Danny

It would seem that Briana and Justin have vastly different experiences and needs when it comes to being on time for important things. An adrenaline rushed drive to the airport is a thrill for Justin and something more like torture for Briana. However, there is a breakdown in how they are communicating and responding to one another's needs. Either Briana is not being clear about how and when she needs to get to places, or Justin is not hearing and responding to her messages well enough to meet her needs. As a result, Briana has decided that she needs to meet her own needs independently rather than trusting Justin to meet them. Unfortunately, this act of mistrust will only hurt their connection.

If Briana wants to build trust with Justin, she needs to let him know the truth of how his actions affect her: "I feel scared and stressed when you cut things so close that we have to speed to the airport and risk missing our flight. I need to feel safe and secure about getting to the airport and other important appointments on time." If Justin cares about building trust with Briana, then he will take this great information and adjust to meet her needs. He can also be honest and vulnerable with Briana about his need for thrills. By exchanging the truth about their needs, this couple can build a plan for meeting one another's needs in a way that protects their connection and makes them feel known, protected, and trusted.

> Most of us are scared to be hurt or controlled in our relationships, therefore being vulnerable and revealing our feelings and needs is counter-intuitive, but it is also one of the most effective ways to build lasting intimacy. Knowing the truth sets us free. Exchanging the truth will help us deepen levels of trust.

KYLO in Action

1. What do I need in my close relationships?

2. How can I be more vulnerable and honest about communicating my feelings and needs?

3) How can I strengthen trust with those I love and share how they're affecting me—both positively and negatively?

_____

_____

_____

4) Talk with someone this week and share what's going on inside of you using an "I message." Write down how it went and how you felt in sharing.

"I feel _____ when _____ and

     emotion   describe experience

I need to feel _____ ."

           emotion

_____

_____

_____

_____

_____

Remember: *Keep Your Love On!*

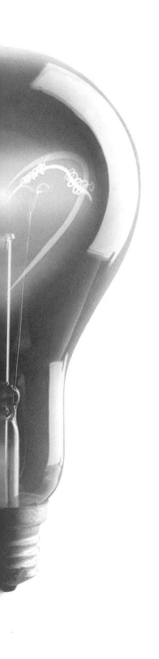

LESSON 7
Communicating in Conflict

Communicating the message, "I care about your needs," at the beginning of a respectful conversation is crucial. The next step is discovering the need through the process of sending and receiving clear messages to one another. In order for this process to be successful, you must have both a speaker and a listener. If either component is missing, you have silence or a collective monologue, not a conversation.

(Keep Your Love On!, page 115)

Core Concepts

Read Chapter 7 of the *Keep Your Love On* book, listen to Session 7 of the audio series, and/or watch DVD Session 7. Then fill in the blanks below.

Preparing for Conflict

- When you have a relationship with another human being, _____ is going to happen.

- The way you communicate and resolve conflict will either weaken or _____ a relational connection.

- Conflict becomes ugly when you _____ out of fear and pain.

- Two people who are disconnected are not going to "work things out," they are only going to try to _____ one another to get their needs met.

- The key is to prioritize the _____ above the issue, offense, confusion, or disagreement.

- Be prepared to _____ to meet the needs of the other person.

Guidelines for Communication

- Communicating the message, "I care about your _____," at the beginning of a respectful conversation to resolve conflict is crucial.

- In a respectful conversation, there must always be a speaker and a _____.

- The role of the listener (TV) is to _____ what the speaker (DVD player) is saying.

- A skilled listener with a servant's _____ is the deadliest weapon against the fear-bombs that threaten connection.

Core Concepts Key Words:

heart	needs	adjust	strengthen	conflict
understand	listener	connection	react	control/manipulate

Think About It

1) Have you ever prioritized an issue above a relationship? Based on what you have learned, what are some ways you could have handled the situation differently?

2) Have you ever tried to work out a problem while disconnected from the other person? How did it go?

3) What is your boundary for engaging in disrespectful conversations? Do you typically react to the other person's fear and pain in the same vein, or do you respond and invite the person to a respectful conversation?

4) When you need to express a need and ask the other person to adjust, how hard is it for you to believe that he or she cares about meeting your need? Conversely, when someone comes to you with a need, how hard is it for you to care about meeting his or her need?

5) In a confrontation, do you have the goal of listening to understand and finding out the person's need, or do you focus on trying to get the other person to agree with you and protecting yourself?

Real Life Scenario

David and Mark

As the staff meeting broke up, David approached Mark, his long-time friend and one of the three founding partners of their business. "Do you think we could meet in my office for a minute?"

"If it's all right with you, I'd like to stay in here," Mark said, closing his laptop. "I've got another meeting in ten minutes."

"Okay," David agreed, sitting down to face him. "I'd really like to end the Cold War we've been having for the last three weeks."

Mark nodded stiffly. "Yeah, that would be nice. Unfortunately I really don't know what to say that we haven't already said. You've made it clear that you don't think what you did was a problem."

"And nothing you've said has convinced me otherwise," David affirmed. "I really wish you could look at the situation more objectively. I know Kent is your friend, but as his employer, I saw things very differently. You already knew I had to confront him several times over the last year. Nothing changed—he just kept doing whatever he wanted. He never listened to what I had to say and was more than disrespectful to me."

"So you fired him behind my back while I was on a business trip."

"It was my call to make," David said firmly. "He was my department."

"And you knew he was my friend. You knew that he needed this job. We agreed when we started this business that we would make the important decisions together. You wouldn't have fired him if I had been here."

"Firing a junior employee in my department is not a partner matter, Mark. I would never interfere if you were firing one of your employees."

"And I would never be rude enough to fire someone you're close to without consulting you," Mark retorted bitterly. "Until we agree about that I think the Cold War still stands."

David sighed. "Please don't make this a bigger deal than it is, Mark. We go back twenty years. Let's work it out."

"My next appointment is here," Mark said, standing. "Let's finish this another time."

? What *is* the Problem?

What are Mark and David's goals in this interaction? What is the priority for each of them—the issue or their connection?

How could Mark and David listen and communicate more effectively to resolve this conflict?

David and Mark strongly disagree over David's decision to fire Mark's friend. Multiple conversations have only entrenched them further in defending their conflicting views, and they are allowing this disagreement to take priority over protecting their connection.

Resolution is only possible if they first choose to put their connection above the problem. In order to do this, they must change the goal in communication from agreeing with one another to understanding one another. Then they must have a respectful conversation in which they take turns communicating how the other person's behavior is affecting them.

Mark needs to unpack his offense with David and put it in terms of feelings and needs. For example: "When you as my business partner make a decision that profoundly affects the life of someone I care about without involving me, I feel disrespected, hurt, and unsafe. In a situation in which both business and personal relationships are involved, I need to feel that my voice matters and will be heard."

David's first job will be to listen well and affirm Mark's feelings and needs. Then they can switch roles and David can share about his needs as an employer. Ideally they will be able to take this information and create an effective solution for resolving the disagreement and/or avoiding future disagreements. But even if they ultimately continue to disagree, they can agree that they won't disconnect over the issue again, and that they are commited to protecting their connection.

> When you make your goal to protect connection, conflict becomes an opportunity to strengthen your most important relationships. Ask yourself a few questions: "Am I aware of my goal going into confrontation? What is the strength of my connection with this person right now? Do I understand what they need from me?" Make it a point to practice your listening and communication skills. Make connection your goal—it may be your greatest investment.

KYLO in Action

1) How strong is your relational connection plan? Consider where you need to:
   - Strengthen the cords of connection.
   - Start respectful conversations by clarifying that you care deeply about the other person's needs.
   - Send and receive clear messages.
   - Refuse to participate in conversation with someone who doesn't want to be respectful too.
   - Choose to keep your love on, destroy fear, believe the best about people, and trust them to care.
   - If they don't care, forgive them.
   - Move toward those you love even when it hurts.

   List 1 2 areas of your relational connection plan to focus on this week.

   _____
   _____
   _____
   _____
   _____

2) Think about a person with whom you have a close connection. When was the last time that person asked you for something he or she needed from you? How did you respond? Have you created a strong enough connection where both of you feel comfortable confronting one another? How can you strengthen your connection and assure that

   _____
   _____
   _____
   _____

Remember: *Keep Your Love On!*

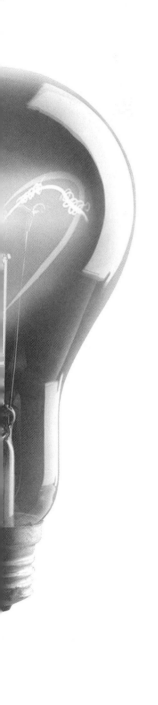

LESSON 8
Levels of Intimacy

> You are responsible to manage different levels of intimacy, responsibility, influence, and trust with people in your life. Likewise, you are responsible to honor the different levels of access and influence others allow you to have in their lives. These levels are absolutely righteous, healthy, normal, and good. It is supposed to be like this! It has to be like this.

(Keep Your Love On!, page 124)

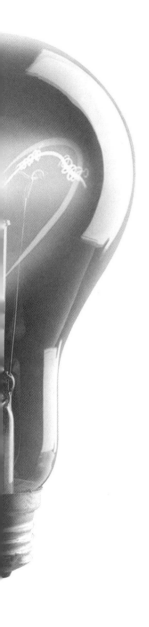

Core Concepts

Read Chapter 8 of the *Keep Your Love On* book, listen to Session 8 of the audio series, and/or watch DVD Session 8. Then fill in the blanks below.

Levels of Intimacy

- The more intimacy you have with someone, the more _____ you give the person to your energy, time, and resources.

- You need to cultivate and protect your levels of intimacy. When people become disrespectful or violate your trust, you need to _____ them out to a place of access that they can handle.

- The innermost circle is your _____ . Some people like to call this the "God Spot."

- The next level of intimacy is for your most intimate human relationship, your deepest soul tie. *Only* _____ *person* is going to fit into that spot. If you are married, this should be your spouse. If you are unmarried, this person could be a friend, a parent, a sibling, or even a business partner.

- The next circle out contains people like _____ or grandkids, followed by extended family and close friends.

- The further out the levels, the more people can fit in them.

Boundaries

- Boundaries communicate _____ .

- When you don't put boundaries around something, you _____ disrespectful relationships.

- Desperate people will put a _____ on you to get what they need, so you need to be able to protect your resources.

- In order to say "yes" to your _____, you must be willing to say "no" to other things along the way.

- The biggest "yes" is saying yes to _____. It is difficult to make and keep boundaries in life if you don't prioritize your relationship with Him.

Core Concepts Key Words:

move	one	core	attract/invite	kids
access	God	value	priorities	demand

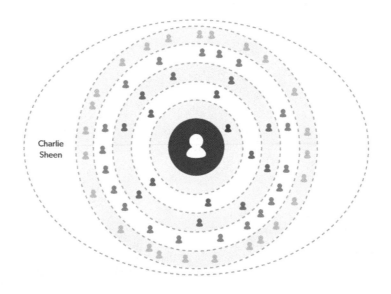

Think About It

1) Who is your closest human relationship? Who belongs in each of the next levels of intimacy?

2) Have you ever been moved further out of someone's circle? Have you moved someone out? Was it necessary? How did it make you feel?

3) Do you allow the needs and demands of other people to pull on your time, energy, and resources too much?

4) Have you ever put a human being in your "God spot," making that person your reason for life and the source of your happiness? How did this affect you?

5) Can you say "no" to people? If not, what does this say about your ability to protect the things you want to say "yes" to?

Sean and Anna

"Hey Danny, can we talk?" Sean asked.

"Sure, what's up?" Danny asked. "How are you and Anna? I can't believe you guys have almost been married a year!"

"Yeah, I know," Sean grinned as he took a seat in Danny's office. "Things are great, I think—I just had a question for you about balancing work and home stuff."

"Okay," Danny nodded encouragingly to the energetic youth pastor.

"There's a kid in the youth group—Jack. He's been coming for almost three years now and we've really connected. His home life is pretty bad, so we've had this setup for a long time where he can call me when he's struggling with something at home. He calls me about once or twice a week and we usually talk for half an hour or so. When we first got married, it didn't seem to bother Anna, but lately she's been getting really annoyed by it."

"Can I ask when Jack usually calls?" Danny asked.

"Well, that's the thing," Sean sighed. "He works the closing shift at a store, so it's normally 9, 10, or sometimes even 11PM."

"Hmmm," Danny's eyebrows rose.

"It's frustrating because he needs my help, but now I know if I take his calls I'm going to hear about it from Anna. I'm not sure what her problem is. She knows Jack's situation and that it's my job to help him."

Why do you think Anna is frustrated with Sean?

How can Sean improve in managing the levels of intimacy in his life?

A Word from Danny

By getting married, Anna and Sean have moved one another into their innermost level of intimacy and prioritized their relationship above all others. However, they are still learning to adjust the level of access other relationships have to their time and energy. Anna is not annoyed with Sean because he's helping Jack, but because she feels that he's taking time and energy out of their relationship "account" to do it. This is sending the message that their relationship doesn't have the same priority to him that it does to her, which feels disrespectful.

Sean and Anna need to have a conversation about their feelings, needs, and expectations for how to prioritize their relationship, agree on what time is "us" time, and commit to setting and keeping boundaries around that. Perhaps Sean can find time to speak with Jack during the workday, or if this isn't an option, he and Anna might agree on a specific evening where Sean can take a call from Jack after work. Whatever plan they come up with can be subject to change, but they must recognize that prioritizing their relationship is not going to happen without their joint commitment, communication, and effort.

> When we don't set boundaries around our relationships, we attract disrespectful relationships into our lives. We must protect what's important to us, and what's important to us are the things we've said 'yes' to. In order to say 'yes' to your priorities, you must say 'no' to other things along the way.

 **KYLO in Action**

1) List 2-3 things you are going to say "yes" to in order to honor the priorities you have set for each of your circles/levels of intimacy:

God:

Spouse/Best Friend:

Children:

Close Friends/Family:

Co-workers:

Community:

World:

2) Take some time to think and pray about where you may struggle to set and keep healthy boundaries in your life. Write down any insights you have.

_____

_____

_____

_____

3) Ask one or two of your closest relationships if they see any adjustments that need to be made in how you're honoring your boundaries and relational priorities. What are you going to do with this valuable information?

_____

_____

_____

_____

Remember: *Keep Your Love On!*

LESSON 9
Guidelines for Setting Boundaries

"When people see how you care for your garden and taste the good fruit of your life, their words and behavior should demonstrate that they recognize your value. If they don't recognize the value of your life and what you have to offer, then you know that you cannot be in a relationship with them. The only people you want to connect yourself with are those who respect the value of your life and their own lives. Only then will your relationships be based on mutual respect and shared fruitfulness."

(Keep Your Love On!, pages 139-140)

Core Concepts

Read Chapter 9 of the *Keep Your Love On* book, listen to Session 9 of the audio series, and/or watch DVD Session 9. Then fill in the blanks below.

Cultivating Your Garden

- God is always sending you love messages. The more you receive His love, the more you will learn to _____ your life as He does.

- By managing what is yours, you will reap a harvest that will nourish you and give you something good to offer others.

- You have to take care of *yourself* before you can take care of someone else.

- The only people you want to connect yourself with are those who _____ the value of your life and their own lives.

Setting Boundaries

- Boundaries keep in what you want to keep in, and keep out what you want to keep out. They protect the _____ of your life—time, energy, resources, and relationships.

- Boundaries *protect* _____ what you value.

- Tell others what *you* _____ are going to do instead of telling them what they have to do.

- Remember that people believe your _____ more than they believe your _____.

- Don't expect people to be _____ when you set limits with them. When your "no" is a "no," it is going to be tested. When your "yes" is a "yes," it is going to be tested.

- When you start telling people what you are going to do and what you're not going to do and follow through on both, people will come to _____ what you say.

Core Concepts Key Words:

value	priorities	yourself	communicate	actions
respect	happy	you	words	believe

1) What practices have you established—or should you establish—to remind you of your value, priorities, and purpose?

2) Have you ever allowed the demands of others to move you away from your priorities? Describe what happened. How could you have responded differently to that situation as a powerful person?

3) Have you ever struggled with bitterness over feeling used and exploited by "consumers"—those who consistently demand your time, energy, or resources without giving anything back? If so, how could this be affecting your current life and relationships?

4) Are you currently taking more responsibility for someone else's life, problems, and/or choices than you should? What do you need to do to release that person to be powerful and responsible for himself or herself?

plan for our kids

Real Life Scenario

Kelly and Cheryl

"Hey Kelly, do you think you could stay till 7 or 8 again tonight? We really need to get that newsletter out by tomorrow."

"Sure," Kelly answered, smiling at Cheryl. Inside, anxiety coursed through her. This was the third time her new boss had asked her to stay late that week. She had planned to spend the evening catching up on a big grad school project, but Kelly decided she would just have to do it over the weekend, even though it meant missing church again. It was just one week, she told herself, and she needed the extra money.

Over the next month, Cheryl kept finding things around the office that she desperately needed Kelly to do "just this once." Kelly enjoyed feeling helpful and liked the higher paychecks she got from putting in extra hours…but then she opened the envelope with her midterm grades. They were lower than they'd ever been.

Kelly promised herself that she'd cut back on work and focus on grad school. But before she could tell her boss, Cheryl asked if Kelly would take over a project for a client. Kelly immediately said, "I'll do it!" As stressed as she was, she was flattered that Cheryl wanted her, and was sure that Cheryl would pay her the much higher rates she charged for such a project. For three weeks, Kelly worked every night and weekend and skipped the gym, church, hangouts with friends and even a test to make Cheryl's deadline. The morning after she turned in the project, she woke up with a nasty cold. As she lay in bed, miserable and overwhelmed by the thought of the classes she was missing, she comforted herself with the thought that next week's paycheck would be twice what she normally made.

When Kelly left Cheryl's office and opened her check envelope on payday, however, what she saw shocked her. Cheryl had only paid Kelly her normal assistant rate for the project. "I can't believe this!" Kelly said aloud. "She's using me!"

? What *is* the Problem?

What is problematic with the way Kelly is managing her priorities and boundaries?

_____

_____

_____

What should Kelly do to protect her "garden" and set healthy boundaries with Cheryl?

_____

_____

_____

_____

💬 A Word from Danny

Kelly is working for a consumer. Cheryl will gladly consume all the time, effort, and skill Kelly will give her, without making sure her demands are fair and don't conflict with Kelly's other priorities. After just a few months of not setting limits with Cheryl, Kelly's studies, health, and personal life are all being seriously threatened, and she is feeling disrespected and exploited. If Kelly hopes to save her life and her job, she needs to remember that it is her responsibility to manage the health of her garden and protect her priorities, not Cheryl's or anyone else's. She needs to reconnect to the God-given value of her goals, dreams, time, skills, and health, and commit to honoring that value by setting clear, healthy boundaries around them—boundaries she will keep no matter what anyone else does.

With her priorities clear, Kelly can rebuild the "budget" for where the resources of her life need to go. If school is her main commitment right now, class time and generous study hours should be firmly off-limits to anyone or anything else. After that, she can take a fresh look at how to balance work hours with time for taking care of her physical, emotional, relational and spiritual health. She should also nail down what she needs to feel fairly compensated for her work.

The final and greatest test for Kelly will be acting on her plan. She not only needs to be powerful enough to let Cheryl know that she is only available for X hours a week and expects fair rates for projects—she needs to be ready for Cheryl to push back on those limits. If Cheryl refuses to respect Kelly's limits, Kelly should be ready to find another job.

> Just because you set boundaries doesn't mean that you don't care deeply for people. Boundaries are one of the best ways to communicate love and value to the people around you. Remember, people believe your actions more than they believe your words. So the more consistently people encounter the boundaries you've set in your life, the more they can trust that it is you that manages your life. The time, energy, and access you give them communicates true value in your relationship.

KYLO in Action

1) Spend some time thinking about the "garden" God has given you. Rate the health of each area on a scale of 1-5 (5 being healthiest) and choose a few areas you want to cultivate to make healthier and more fruitful.

- physical health
- emotional health
- mental health
- spiritual health
- education
- talents
- gifts
- callings
- finances
- relationships

2) Focus this week on maintaining a successful offense in keeping your boundaries. When you tell someone what you are going to do, ask yourself:

   • Am I making this choice to protect my priorities?
   • Am I making sure that I am only telling this person what I will do and not telling them what they need to do?
   • Will I honestly be okay no matter what he/she does?

3) Do you recognize any area of your life where someone is being disrespectful or irresponsible with your time and resources? Decide to set some limits and respectfully communicate your priorities to them with clear and powerful statements about what you are going to do. Above all, *do what you say you are going to do.*

Remember: *Keep Your Love On!*

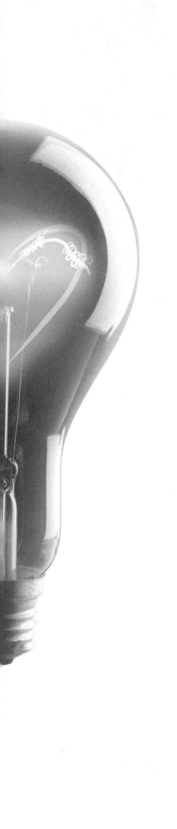

LESSON 10
Did You Learn to Love?

The whole nature of relationship is that you cannot control it. All you can control is your free choice to love others and receive their love. When you make this choice, freedom grows and fear goes. The sign that you really have love in your relationships is that you and the people around you are free and not scared. Free people are going to tell you the truth. They are going to make mistakes. That *will* test the relationship and the state of your heart. It will require you to grow up and become powerful.

(*Keep Your Love On!*, page 156)

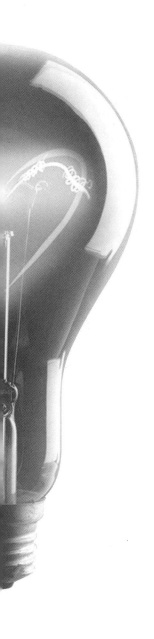

Core Concepts

Read Chapter 10 of the *Keep Your Love On* book, listen to Session 10 of the audio series, and/or watch DVD Session 10. Then fill in the blanks below.

Jesus Loves Sinners

- If we want to reflect the love of *Jesus* to the world, we need to learn to keep our love on with sinners.

- It's hard to go out and love sinners like Jesus did when you're still _____ of your own sin.

- Jesus didn't create distance with broken people; He created *boundaries*.

- By solving the _____ problem, Jesus created a safe place—the safest place in the world—for us to be loved, known, accepted, and forgiven.

- The _____ separates us from our mess every time, no matter how big.

Loving the World

- Loving others is the sign that we _____ God.

- Our spiritual calling is nothing less than to love and to be loved by God and people.

- You cannot control relationships. The only thing you can control is your free _____ to love others and receive their love.

- The sign that you really have love in your relationships is that you and the people around you are _____ .

- People who really know God can do shocking, powerful things—they can _____ people that many would declare unforgivable and impossible to love.

- If we're going to keep the one big commandment He gave us—to love as He loves—then we need bigger _____ .

Core Concepts Key Words:

choice	God	know	sin	afraid
connection	cross	hearts	free	love

Think About It

1) Do you struggle at all with the fear of failure or the belief that it's not okay for you to have visible problems?

2) Are you at all afraid to be known or feel the need to hide parts of your life from those closest to you? How willing are you to come "into the light"?

3) Think of a time when you struggled to keep your love on with someone who hurt or disappointed you. What did you ultimately choose and what was the result?

4) Think of a time when you made a mess and someone in your life kept his/her love on with you? How did that affect you?

Mark and Julie

"What you've heard is true, Danny," Mark managed through tears. "I've been having an affair with one of my interns for about three months. I did this once twelve years ago, when Julie and I were on staff at another church. I confessed to the congregation and swore I'd never do it again. Yet here I am." He shook his head in grief and shame.

Danny let Mark weep for a moment, and then asked, "So Mark, what do you think is the problem?"

The problem, Danny knew, was not the mess Mark had made, huge as it was. The problem was the broken spot in his heart that had created the mess. Over the next half hour, Danny helped Mark uncover the core problem in his life. Growing up in church, Mark had received the message that Christian leaders weren't supposed to have any problems. This bred a huge fear of failure and fear of being known, which led him into a lifestyle of hiding and isolation. Even in his most intimate relationship with his wife, his fear had prevented him from being able to connect deeply with her. That disconnection had created a huge vacuum in his heart, and he'd fallen for the offer of counterfeit intimacy outside marriage. After the first affair, he'd tried desperately to keep his behavior in line, but never really dealt with the fear and isolation ruling his heart. And so he'd ended up again in the very situation he'd always feared—having a massive failure in public.

"So we've found the broken spot," Danny affirmed. "The next question is, what are you going to do about it and the mess it's led you to make?"

Mark looked soberly up at Danny. "Well, I want to believe that God can heal me and help me clean up the mess."

"I want to believe that too," Danny nodded. "Who would you say has been affected by this mess? Whose trust has been broken?"

Mark wept profusely as he went down the list. His wife. His three children. Their extended families. His staff team and the congregation. As a leader, he had influence with a lot of people, all of whom had been hurt by his poor choices. But when he left Danny's office, Mark was determined to do whatever it took to clean up his mess with everyone on that list. He didn't know how long it would take or what life would look like on the other side. But he had been given a chance to make things right—and he would take it.

What are some of the things that probably kept Mark from recognizing and dealing with the "broken spot" in his life?

How did Danny and Mark keep their love on and act like powerful people in this interaction? How might the outcome in Mark's life be different because Danny helped Mark get to the heart issues and empowered him to clean up his mess, rather than punishing his behavior?

Remember: *Keep Your Love On!*

A Word from Danny

Two years after Mark's tear-and-truth-filled meeting with me, I asked him and his wife Julie to share their journey of restoration with a group of church leaders. I wanted these leaders to see an example of what it can look like when a Christian community keeps its love on and empowers someone—particularly a leader—to clean up a relational mess.

"I've done punishment and I've done discipline, and I'll tell you that discipline is way harder," Mark declared honestly. "It's much harder to actually clean up your mess and deal with the heart problem that caused it." He went on to describe how he had met with every single person on his list—the senior pastor, members of the pastoral staff, family members, and many members of the congregation—to apologize and rebuild trust. Some forgave him quickly, while others obviously struggled to relate to him after what he had done. "I had to do my part to and then trust God to bring healing to these relationships," Mark explained.

"After meeting with everyone involved, my priority was learning to live in the light," he went on. In order to break his old habit of hiding his problems and living in isolation, Mark set about establishing relationships in which he allowed people to see what was really going on inside him, and began seeing a counselor on an indefinite basis.

"I will pay money for the rest of my life to have a man know everything that's going on in my life and giving me godly input," Mark stated. "It feels really healthy to have people know who I am."

Chief among those who have gotten to know the real Mark are his wife and three children. Their heart-to-heart connections have gone to a far deeper level now that fear is not shutting down his ability to show them his feelings and flaws. Each one of them has joined him "in the light," where they are free to communicate their feelings, raise concerns, and finally meet one another's needs as a family.

Mark insisted that he would only return to pastoral leadership when he felt that his relationships with his wife and family were strong and healthy. When, after a year, he and Julie told the congregation what God had done to restore and transform their marriage, they were celebrated with victory chants, shouts, and tears of joy. By the next fall, Mark had returned to his pastoral role, and continues to transparently shared his journey with those he leads.

As I walked through this process with Mark and Julie, I saw just how many opportunities they had to say, "This is too hard." They—and our whole community—were required to be powerful and keep their love on in a way they never had before. Most people don't sign up for that challenge in the face of their mistakes. But they did, and every part of their life has been restored and transformed into something stronger, healthier, and more powerful, which brings hope to all of us. May we all rise to the same challenge and receive the same hope!

1) How would you answer if you were asked, "Have you learned to love?"

Thank you for choosing KYLO Series Study Guide.
Find us at *Amazon.com* to leave a review of your
experience.

Loving on Purpose Ministries on Facebook:
Facebook.com/LovingOnPurpose

Other Loving on Purpose Resources

Love is a choice.
Learn to love on purpose at
lovingonpurpose.com

NOTES

A FRESH, FREEDOM-BASED PERSPECTIVE ON PARENTING

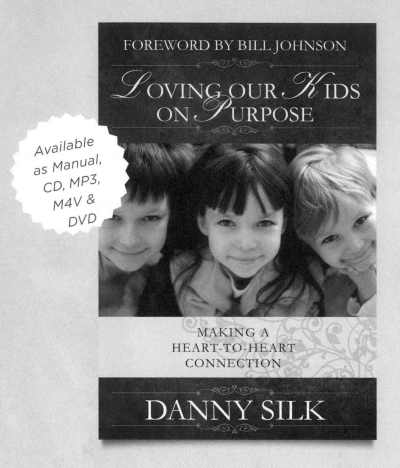

FOREWORD BY BILL JOHNSON

Loving Our Kids on Purpose

MAKING A
HEART-TO-HEART
CONNECTION

DANNY SILK

Available as Manual, CD, MP3, M4V & DVD

Loving Our Kids On Purpose brings fresh perspective to the age-old role of parenting. Through teaching, storytelling and humor, Danny shares his personal family stories as well as numerous experiences he's had helping other families. You will learn to:

- Protect your heart-to-heart connection with your children
- Teach your children to manage increasing levels of freedom
- Replace the tools of intimidation and control
- Create a safe place for children to build confidence and personal responsibility

View this and more at lovingonpurpose.com

READY FOR MARRIAGE? DANNY EQUIPS YOU FOR THE "BIG" CONVERSATION

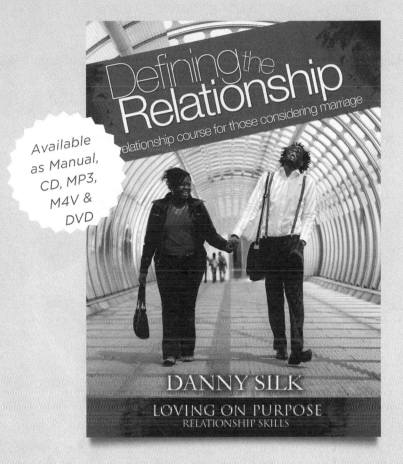

Many Christian couples come to a point where they must "Define their Relationship." In this series, Danny's comedic style of teaching will inspire, challenge, and bring couples into a serious reality check about their decision toward marriage. The goal of this series is to impart COURAGE—the courage to either push through the rugged realities of a loving relationship or the courage to walk away. Whether you are single, dating, or already engaged, this course will teach you how to love on purpose.

View this and more at lovingonpurpose.com

WHAT IS HONOR AND HOW DO YOU PRACTICE IT?

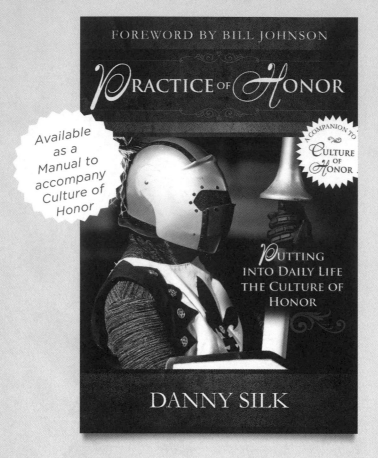

The *Practice of Honor* manual is a practical resource for those who have read *Culture of Honor* by Danny Silk and for leaders, individuals, or those who desire to learn how to cultivate a culture of honor in their sphere of influence. Based on the revival culture of Bethel Church in Redding, California, it is a template to help any leader develop an environment that brings out the very best in people. It is a recipe for introducing the Spirit of God—His freedom—and how to host and embrace that freedom as a community of believers.

View this and more at lovingonpurpose.com

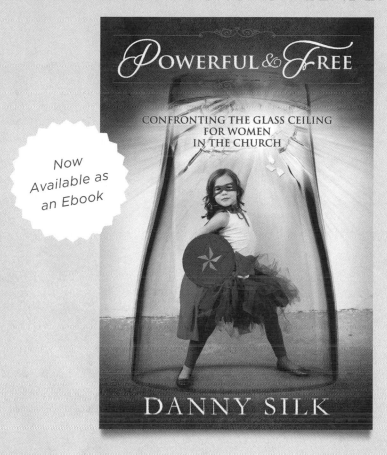